Be a
METEOROLOGIST

BY KRISTEN RAJCZAK

Gareth Stevens
PUBLISHING

Please visit our website, www.garethstevens.com. For a free color catalog of all our high-quality books, call toll free 1-800-542-2595 or fax 1-877-542-2596.

Library of Congress Cataloging-in-Publication Data

Rajczak, Kristen.
Be a meteorologist / by Kristen Rajczak.
 p. cm. — (Be a scientist!)
Includes index.
ISBN 978-1-4824-1210-9 (pbk.)
ISBN 978-1-4824-1197-3 (6-pack)
ISBN 978-1-4824-1442-4 (library binding)
1. Meteorology — Vocational guidance — Juvenile literature. 2. Meteorologists — Juvenile literature.
I. Rajczak, Kristen. II. Title.
QC869.5 R35 2015
551.5023—d23

First Edition

Published in 2015 by
Gareth Stevens Publishing
111 East 14th Street, Suite 349
New York, NY 10003

Designer: Katelyn E. Reynolds
Editor: Therese Shea

Photo credits: Cover, pp. 1, 29 John Tlumacki/The Boston Globe/Getty Images; cover, pp. 1–32 (background texture), 22 NOAA/Getty Images; p. 4 Ingram Publishing/Thinkstock.com; p. 5 Image Source/Getty Images; p. 6 SCIENCE SOURCE/Photo Researchers/Getty Images; p. 7 U.S. Navy/Time Life Pictures/Getty Images; pp. 9, 14, 15, 26 Joe Raedle/Getty Images; p. 10 Jim Edds/Photo Researchers/Getty Images; p. 11 Mark Elias/Bloomberg/Getty Images; p. 13 Craig F. Walker/The Denver Post/Getty Images; p. 16 NASA/Getty Images; p. 17 Ricardo R. Guzman/U.S. Navy/Getty Images; p. 19 Jonathan Daniel/Getty Images; p. 20 Chris Condon/Getty Images; p. 21 Jonathan Saruk/The Weather Channel/Getty Images; p. 23 HO/AFP/Getty Images; p. 24 fonikum/iStock Vectors/Getty Images; p. 25 Gines Romero/Shutterstock.com; p. 27 Christina Petersen/Getty Images.

Printed in the United States of America

CPSIA compliance information: Batch #CS15GS: For further information contact Gareth Stevens, New York, New York at 1-800-542-2595.

CONTENTS

Words in the glossary appear in **bold** type the first time they are used in the text.

A CALL FOR RAIN

Have you ever been disappointed by the weather forecast on the evening news? Maybe it's calling for rain the day of your soccer match. The weather map has a big blob of green that seems to be moving straight toward your town, just like the one on the next page.

WHAT IS METEOROLOGY?

Forecasting the weather is just one part of a meteorologist's job. Meteorologists are scientists who study Earth's atmosphere. The science of meteorology examines the causes of and changes in weather and climate. Meteorologists are also concerned with how people's activities affect Earth's atmosphere.

If the match is still a few days away, don't worry yet. Earth's atmosphere is constantly changing, which means the forecast can, too. It's a meteorologist's job to keep an eye on these changes by measuring conditions in the atmosphere. Meteorologists use that knowledge, plus past experience, to guess what could happen in the future.

This TV weather forecaster, also known as a weathercaster, is standing in front of a weather map that shows areas of green, which mean rain!

People have been interested in the weather for thousands of years. By the 1600s, scientists had already begun to record wind direction and rainfall measurements. The thermometer was invented around 1600, as well as the barometer, which measures **atmospheric pressure**.

By the 1800s, even more meteorological tools had been invented to help scientists make sense of the weather around them. They began to understand that weather moves in systems across Earth, and this allowed them to do limited forecasting. When the **telegraph** was introduced, weather reports could be sent anywhere instantly. The skills of meteorologists have only become more valuable over time.

METEOROLOGICA

The term "meteorology" comes from a Greek word meaning "something that happens high in the sky." The ancient Greeks tried to understand how clouds, wind, and rain worked together. Aristotle, a great thinker in ancient Greece, wrote a book called *Meteorologica* more than 2,000 years ago. It included his studies of Earth's atmosphere.

Aristotle

Military operations during World War II (1939-1945) depended on knowledge of the weather. It was for this reason that great advances in meteorological **technology** occurred at this time, including **radar**.

7

IT STARTS WITH SCHOOL

Are you curious about Earth's atmosphere? Does learning to forecast the weather interest you? Are you good in your math and science classes in school? If you answered yes to these questions, then you should think about becoming a meteorologist!

WHAT ELSE SHOULD YOU KNOW?

Meteorologists work a lot with computers, so being knowledgeable about new technology is a good idea if you want to study meteorology. Speaking a foreign language, such as French, Russian, or German, can be helpful, too. Meteorologists often look at research from other parts of the world. They may work with people around the globe, too.

The first step to becoming a meteorologist is doing well in school. In high school, you should take all the math and science classes you can, especially **physics**, Earth science, and an advanced math class called calculus. These classes will help you once you begin studying in college—and a college degree is a requirement for meteorologists.

Part of the American Meteorological Society's definition of a meteorologist states that a meteorologist is a person with "specialized education." That means you have to study to be this special kind of scientist.

Some colleges offer degrees in meteorology. But many meteorologists have college degrees in atmospheric science, computer science, math, and physics. They choose to take classes that teach them about oceanography, or the study of the oceans, and other important topics involved in meteorology.

STAY IN SCHOOL!

Meteorologists who want to do scientific research commonly must have more than just a college degree. They need to go to graduate school to earn a master's degree or, even higher, a doctoral degree. In graduate school, they choose a certain type of meteorology to specialize in, such as agricultural meteorology.

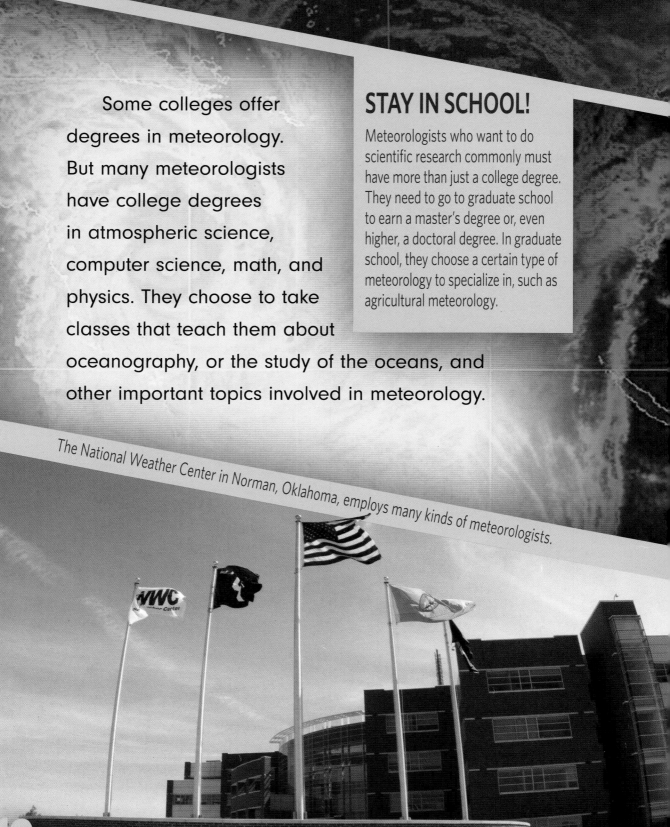

The National Weather Center in Norman, Oklahoma, employs many kinds of meteorologists.

NATIONAL WEATHER CENTER

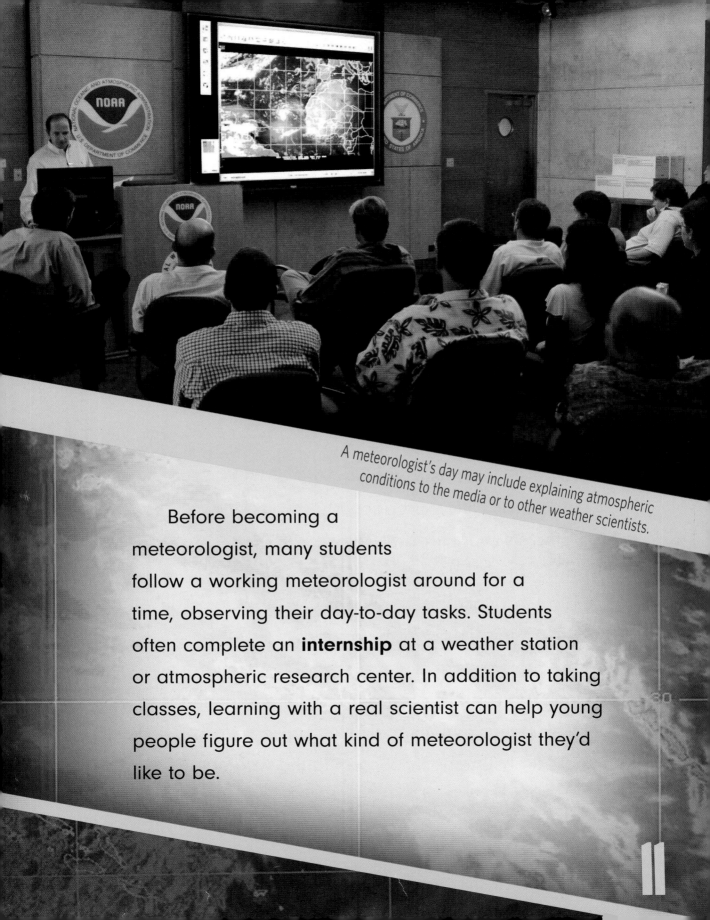

A meteorologist's day may include explaining atmospheric conditions to the media or to other weather scientists.

Before becoming a meteorologist, many students follow a working meteorologist around for a time, observing their day-to-day tasks. Students often complete an **internship** at a weather station or atmospheric research center. In addition to taking classes, learning with a real scientist can help young people figure out what kind of meteorologist they'd like to be.

TYPES OF METEOROLOGISTS

The meteorologist you're probably most familiar with is called a broadcast meteorologist. They work at TV and radio stations explaining the weather forecast for others to understand. People depend on broadcast meteorologists' reports to plan their outdoor activities. Broadcast meteorologists are especially needed because they're the ones who warn the public about extreme weather, such as **tornadoes**, snowstorms, or **hurricanes**.

Some meteorologists go to school for engineering. That would be a great area of study for someone looking to become an instrument specialist. These scientists design new tools and systems for recording the weather.

NOT ALL WEATHERCASTERS

People who report the weather aren't necessarily meteorologists. Some weathercasters simply pass on weather reports they've received from forecasting services, such as the National Weather Service (NWS). They may have gone to school for broadcast journalism, which teaches them skills such as public speaking, but don't have much of a science background.

Some meteorologists don't want to be on camera. It takes an outgoing personality as well as forecasting knowledge to be a broadcast meteorologist.

Research meteorologists commonly focus on a certain topic, such as clouds or hurricanes. They spend their time gathering measurements and other facts and figures, or data, about their area of research in order to learn more and make new discoveries.

One type of research meteorologist is a climatologist. Climatologists study climate using weather records from past years. They look for changes over time and **predict** future trends. Archive meteorologists also look at past weather records to make sure they're as **accurate** and detailed as possible.

After working as a scientist for many years, a meteorologist may teach at a college or high school. Sometimes they combine this role with research.

These meteorologists are tracking a hurricane at the National Hurricane Center in Miami, Florida.

15

SERVING OUR COUNTRY

The government is the largest employer of meteorologists in the United States. Many work for the National Oceanic and Atmospheric Administration (NOAA) or the National Aeronautics and Space Administration (NASA).

Meteorologists are also a very important part of the US military. Knowing the weather and sea conditions and how they might change is a central part of planning military missions. Meteorologists are stationed at US military bases all over the world. They even work on ships at sea!

The US Department of Agriculture hires meteorologists, too. These scientists forecast growing conditions for farmers.

NASA NEEDS TO KNOW

Over time, NASA meteorologists have discovered that even slight cloud cover can affect how a rocket will take off. Their job is a real challenge, too. They need to know what the weather will be like at an exact time and location, not just generally over a few hours in an area.

NASA launch

In the US military, the weather can help decide whether troops will jump out of a plane! Strong winds can blow troops off course as they're falling.

17

IMPORTANT INFORMATION

Construction businesses, transportation companies, and fishermen all might use meteorologists' knowledge to prepare for changing conditions. If a business is large enough, it may employ its own meteorologist. Others use private forecasting companies that hire meteorologists to forecast the weather and then sell that knowledge to companies and people that want it.

Did you know that professional football teams use a weather service? The New York Jets, Baltimore Ravens, and Philadelphia Eagles get their weather reports from the meteorologists at a company called WeatherWorks. These scientists also work with lawyers in court cases about weather-related injuries or property damage.

NATIONAL WEATHER SERVICE

The forecasters we see on the news often get their weather reports from the National Weather Service. It's part of NOAA. The National Weather Service's mission is to "provide weather, water, and climate data, forecasts and warnings for the protection of life and property and enhancement of the national economy."

It's common for National Football League games to still take place when it's snowing. You can see snow on the field during this game at Lambeau Field in Green Bay, Wisconsin. Lightning, however, is considered too dangerous for the players and fans.

19

Whether they're working for the government or a private company, meteorologists commonly work in weather stations and observation centers. They collect data and **satellite** reports to make short-term and long-term forecasts. The cool thing about being a meteorologist is that every day is different—because the weather is!

WATCHING FOR BAD WEATHER

Meteorologists are the first line of defense against severe weather as they're the ones who often see it coming. The National Weather Service issues "watches" if the conditions are right for bad weather, such as thunderstorms that could cause power outages or floods. "Warnings" are issued when that weather event is actually occurring in an area.

National Weather Service Weather Forecast Offices have meteorologists on duty 24 hours a day every day of the year. That's because the weather doesn't stop just because it's night in one part of the world! There's at least one short-term forecaster who's working on the weather for the next 1 to 2 days. A long-term forecaster is also on duty looking further ahead.

Don't blame a meteorologist if the forecast is wrong! The slightest change in the atmosphere can turn a short rainstorm into several inches of snow.

21

HIGH-TECH TOOLS

Today's meteorologists use advanced technology to study the weather. Radar, which stands for **ra**dio **d**etection **a**nd **r**anging, finds and measures precipitation. Doppler radar is a special kind of radar used to measure wind speed and direction.

COMPUTING THE WEATHER

Meteorologists use some of the fastest and most powerful computers in the world. Different weather conditions are entered into a computer so it can create models of weather systems. The models then make weather "happen" on the computer. This allows meteorologists to see what might happen days or weeks into the future!

Satellites are placed high in the atmosphere so they can capture photos of large hurricanes such as this one.

These are NOAA's WP-3D Orion aircraft. NOAA operates within the US Department of Commerce.

Satellites orbiting in Earth's atmosphere allow meteorologists to see weather systems moving around the planet. Early weather satellites could only show pictures, but today, satellites can also monitor wind speed, temperature, and other atmospheric conditions.

Specially equipped aircraft can fly right into weather systems. They've flown into hailstorms, hurricanes, and even the smoke and heat produced by a **volcanic eruption**!

CREATING THE FORECAST

Whether it's for the military, a football team, or just regular people, all different kinds of meteorologists work together to forecast the weather. Here's how the weather forecast gets from them to you:

1. **Weather observers record measurements about four times a day at weather stations on land and at sea all over the world. More than 500 weather stations release weather balloons into the atmosphere to collect data higher above Earth's surface.**

2. **Data is sent to world weather centers in Russia, the United States, and Australia. Computers put the facts together to give a good picture of the global weather.**

ACCURACY

In the last few decades, weather forecast accuracy has improved a lot. The 3-day forecasts today are more accurate than 1-day forecasts 20 years ago. Meteorologists' 5-day forecasts are better than 3-day forecasts in 1970! Better technology and more knowledge about how the oceans and atmosphere interact play a big role in this.

We now can get 10-day forecasts and even hourly forecasts on cell phones and websites.

25

3. The National Weather Service in Washington, DC, takes the data and applies it to the United States using computer models.

4. Local weather centers use these models to make even more focused forecasts for certain cities and towns. Broadcast meteorologists or weathercasters also use them to give the forecast on TV or radio.

CLIMATE CHANGE

Meteorologists are some of the scientists working to learn more about global **climate change**, including the slow warming of the atmosphere and oceans. As these changes affect the weather, meteorologists are studying the problems climate change may cause, such as an increase in destructive storms. They're working on solutions to these problems, too.

Meteorologists from all over the world work together so they're better able to predict weather that could cause harm and alert those who could be affected. Just one weather station wouldn't be able to collect enough data to make any weather predictions!

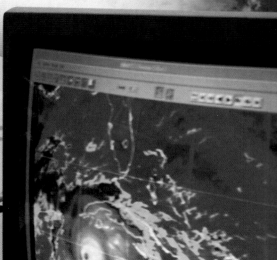

NWS BY THE NUMBERS

number of weather forecast offices	
number of employees	122
number of forecasts per year	5,000
number of warnings per year	1.5 million
number of observations per year	50,000
	76 billion

The National Weather Service doesn't just help you know how to dress for the weather. It helps save lives.

PREDICTING THE FUTURE

In the future, meteorologists will only build on their knowledge and experience—and this can save lives. The more meteorologists research and learn about severe weather, such as hurricanes and tornadoes, the sooner they can warn the public.

POLLUTION PROBLEM

One of the causes of climate change is air pollution. As more nations become industrialized, more pollution from cars, factories, and the burning of fuel like coal will enter the atmosphere. Scientists who understand Earth's atmosphere and how pollution affects it will be in even higher demand in the years to come.

You can start thinking about becoming a meteorologist right now! Working hard in science, math, and computer classes is the first step. Spend time outside observing the world around you. Start taking notes about the daily weather, including the high and low temperatures and other measurable conditions. See if you can find patterns. Then, you'll be on your way to thinking like a meteorologist!

IMPORTANT MOMENTS IN METEOROLOGY

1780 The first international weather observation network is founded in Germany.

1837 Samuel Morse's telegraph makes it possible to send weather reports instantly.

1860 Robert Fitzroy uses telegraph reports and other data to forecast. His forecasts begin to be printed in the newspaper in 1861.

1873 The International Meteorological Organization is founded.

1890 The US Weather Bureau is formed. It becomes the National Weather Service (NWS) in 1970.

1948 The US Air Force Air Weather Service gives the first tornado warning.

1954 The first radar made for meteorological use is introduced.

1960 TIROS I, the first US weather satellite, launches in Florida.

1996 Using Doppler radar, scientists capture a view of an actual tornado.

2007 NWS supercomputers begin making 14 trillion calculations per second.

2012 NWS upgrades its Doppler radars throughout the nation, improving accuracy.

GLOSSARY

accurate: free from mistakes

atmospheric pressure: a downward force caused by the weight of the atmosphere

climate change: long-term change in Earth's climate, caused partly by human activities such as burning oil and natural gas

hurricane: a powerful storm that forms over water and causes heavy rainfall and high winds

internship: a supervised job experience, usually completed by a student

physics: the study of matter, energy, force, and motion, and the relationships among them

predict: to make a guess about what will happen in the future based on knowledge

radar: a way of using radio waves to find distant objects. Also, the machine that uses radio waves to locate and identify objects.

satellite: an object that circles Earth in order to collect and send information

technology: the specialized tools used in an area of study

telegraph: a method of communicating using electric signals sent through wires

tornado: a funnel-shaped cloud of fast winds that often causes destruction

volcanic eruption: the bursting forth of hot, liquid rock from within Earth

FOR MORE INFORMATION

BOOKS

Garbe, Suzanne. *Threatening Skies: History's Most Dangerous Weather.* North Mankato, MN: Capstone Press, 2014.

Gosman, Gillian. *What Do You Know About Weather and Climate?* New York, NY: PowerKids Press, 2014.

Miller, Ron. *Chasing the Storm: Tornadoes, Meteorology, and Weather Watching.* Minneapolis, MN: Twenty-First Century Books, 2014.

WEBSITES

Discovery Kids: Weather
kids.discovery.com/tell-me/curiosity-corner/weather
Find out about predicting weather and how weather conditions occur on the Discovery Kids website.

Weather Wiz Kids
weatherwizkids.com
Learn about many kinds of weather and other information on a website created by a meteorologist just for young people.

INDEX